psalms
of the
heart

a jesuit's journey
through healing

Timothy Brown S.J.

First Edition

Printed in the United States of America

ISBN: 978-1-934074-80-0

Published by Apprentice House

Apprentice House
Communication Department
Loyola University Maryland
4501 N. Charles Street
Baltimore, MD 21210
410.617.5265 • 410.617.2198 (fax)
www.ApprenticeHouse.com
info@ApprenticeHouse.com

to Mary Ellen Whitcomb,
steadfast and loyal

Cover

The painting on the cover was done by Father Joe Kemme of the Society of Jesus.

Joe, a beloved spiritual director and a man of deep prayer, began painting at the age of seventy. His works reflect his deep sense of Christ's suffering and passion. I was honored when he gave me this painting of the Heart of Christ.

table of contents

Our hearts are restless until they rest in Thee.

– St. Augustine

introduction

— Preface —

Several years ago after a heart attack and my fifth stent operation I realized, once again, the importance the Divine Office, and most particularly the Hebrew Psalms, played in my recovery.

Coronary artery disease is a challenge to someone as active as I happen to be. Cardiologists will explain that the arteries supply a constant flow of oxygen enriching blood to the heart.

When arteries are healthy, the smooth, inner lining allows blood to flow freely to the heart, supplying it with nutrients and oxygen. But when arteries begin to get clogged, they narrow to the point where the blood flow is impeded. The arteries become stiff and narrow and all kinds of fat and cholesterol begin accumulating forming plaque deposits. That narrowing and stiffness is called atherosclerosis.

A procedure called angioplasty was developed to remove the built up plaque. This was followed by stenting– a process that opens up clogged arteries and helps to reduce chest pain.

Angioplasty widens and dilates the blocked arteries. The procedure combined with the implantation of stents in the clogged arteries helps to prop open and to decrease the chance of re-blockage.

This procedure saved my life.

I see this book as a reflection on healing– the opening up of all the blocked spiritual arteries of the past years. The Psalms have always been a spiritual way for me to allow the Lord to unblock that which impedes the flow of Christ's grace within me.

I hope that this book has the same spiritual effect on you.

— Timothy Brown

— *Saint Claude la Colombière's prayer* —

I often pray the prayer of the great Jesuit Saint Claude la Colombière:

O God, what will you do to conquer the fearful hardness of our hearts? Lord, you must give us new hearts, tender hearts, sensitive hearts, to replace hearts that are made of marble and of bronze.

You must give us your own heart, Jesus. Come, lovable Heart of Jesus. Place your heart deep in the center of our hearts and enkindle in each heart a flame of love as strong, as great, as the sum of all the reasons that I have for loving you, my God.

O Holy Heart of Jesus, dwell hidden in my heart, so that I may live only in you and only for you, so that, in the end, I may live with you eternally in heaven.

Amen.

—The Inspiration—

I find in times of suffering that the Psalms offer great strength. I use a wonderful volume, The Psalms *with Commentary by Kathleen Norris. In the Introduction to her volume, she writes:*

The God one encounters in the Psalms is God as human beings have experienced him as both awake and asleep, gloriously present and lamentably absent, and above all, various. A warrior who stands up for us, a mother who holds us to her breast. An eagle sheltering us under her wing, and a creator who brings forth lightning, wind, and rain from the storehouse of heaven. The Psalms work in the way that all great poetry works, allowing us to enter no matter who we are or what we believe, or don't believe; addressing us at the deepest level – what Saint Benedict might term "the ear of the heart." (pp. vii, viii)

I found myself drawn to the language of the King James version of the Psalms. Why the King James version, with its lack of inclusive language, you might wonder? Again, Kathleen Norris puts it so well:

One reader of a Jesuit magazine wrote an angry letter to complain about an article that had prominently featured a quotation from John Donne: "No man is an island." The editors commented that since Mr. Donne had died in 1631 they had no means of inviting him to revise his grammar for the more "inclusive" modern era. To read and appreciate seventeenth-century verse, or the King James Bible, one must favor imagination over ideology, and discover for oneself the inclusivity that is there. But this is an increasingly difficult task in our literal-minded age. (p. xiv)

But many poets who write in English regard the King James as the literary standard by which to judge subsequent translations of the Bible. The story of this translation— so called because it was commissioned by King James I of England early in the seventeenth century— is a story about the power and primacy of vivid language and pleasurable speech, words that hold the attention of the ear and provide physical images pleasing to the mind's eye. The translation has so embedded itself into the English language that most people are unaware that many images and phrases still in use entered the idiom through the King James" 'my cup runneth over,' 'all flesh is grass,' 'on eagles' wings,' 'tender mercies,' 'loaves and fishes,' 'lilies of the field,' 'salt of the earth,' 'through a glass, darkly,' 'where your treasure is, there will your heart be also.' (p. xvi)

2011 marks the 400th anniversary of the King James Version of the Bible, *Illustrating the timeless quality of the King James Translation. I ask you to join me in prayer through the Psalms – in imagery that is poetic but not inclusive in the literal sense of the meaning. The images evoked are vivid and provide a great deal of comfort. Join me in your prayer.*

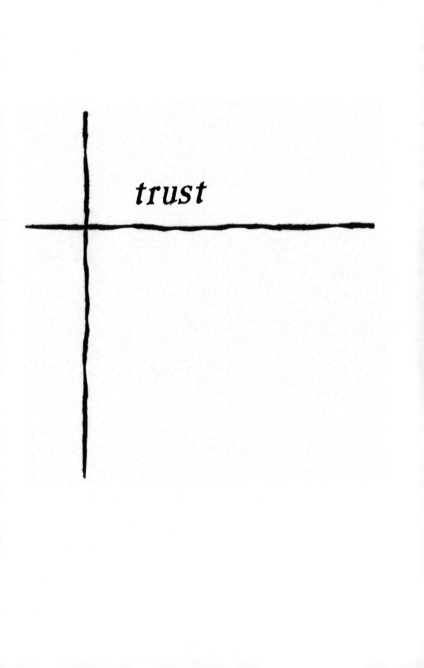

trust

1. I said, I will take heed to my ways, that I sin not with my tongue: I will keep my mouth with a bridle, while the wicked is before me.

2. I was dumb with silence, I held my peace, even from good; and my sorrow was stirred.

3. My heart was hot within me, while I was musing the fire burned: then spake I with my tongue,

4. Lord, make me to know mine end, and the measure of my days, what it is; that I may know how frail I am.

5. Behold, thou hast made my days as an handbreadth; and mine age is as nothing before thee: verily every man at his best stare is altogether vanity.

6. Surely every man walketh in a vain shew: surely they are disquieted in vain: he heapeth up riches, and knoweth not who shall gather them.

7. And now, Lord, what wait I for? My hope is in thee.

—Ecclesiastes 3:11—

God has planted eternity in the human heart.

—Prayer of St. Augustine—

Give me the strength to seek you as you have made me find you, and have given me hope of finding you more and more.

My strength and my weakness are in your hands; preserve the one and heal the other.

My knowledge and my ignorance are in your hands; where you have been closed to me, open to my knocking.

Let me remember you, understand you, love you. Increase these things in me, until you restore me wholly.

Amen.

─── Reflections and Preparations for Advent ───

During my time as Jesuit Provincial of Maryland, I wrote many letters. Here is one I wrote on the feast day of Our Lady of Guadalupe focused on reflections and preparations for the Advent season.

December 12, 2002

Dear Brothers,

You have been in my thoughts and prayers a great deal as we enter fully into this season of Advent. I look forward to my visits with each of you in the coming year. In holding you in my prayers, I want to share with you some reflections for Advent, particularly this beautiful passage about Christ's birth from Caryll Houselander's book, *The Reed of God*:

It was as if the human race were a little dark house, without light or air, locked and latched. The wind of the Spirit had beaten on the door, rattled the windows, tapped on the dark glass with the tiny hands of flowers, flung golden seed against it, even, in hours of storm, lashed it with the boughs of a great tree — the prophesy of the Cross — and yet the Spirit was outside. But one day a girl opened the door, and the little house was swept pure and sweet by the wind. Seas of light swept through it, and the light remained in it; and in that little house a child was born and the Child was God.

This passage may help us see the world a little differently this Advent. During Advent we are waiting. In the words of Simone Weil, "Waiting patiently in expectation is the foundation of the spiritual life." As we wait with the young girl who opened the door for us, I hope that we too say "yes" as Our Lady did. Let each of us use this season to breathe fresh air into our commitment to God — through our thoughts, through our service to one another, through our very ordinary human joys and sorrows.

I have always loved the "O" Antiphons that are sung at vespers during the days preceding Christmas Day. They are the names and the meanings of this child who is both human and divine, whose hand is extended to us with the long reach of hope.

O Wisdom, uttered by the mouth of the Most High,
and reaching to the ends of the earth,
come and teach us the way of prudence.
For the grace of a strong faith to see you
through this season of flu and colds.

O Adonai, ruler of the house of Israel, who appeared
to Moses in the burning bush,
come and redeem us.
For the grace of attention to the ways the Lord
reveals himself to you in these Advent days.

O Root of Jesse, standard of the Nations and of
kings, whom the whole world implores,
come and deliver us.
For the grace of attention to the ways the Lord
reveals himself to you in these Advent days.

O Key of David and Sceptre of the house of Israel,
what you open none can shut,

come and lead us out of darkness.
For the grace of attention to the ways the Lord
reveals himself to you in these Advent days.

O Radiant Dawn, splendor of eternal light and Sun
of justice, shine on those lost in darkness,
come to enlighten us.
For the grace of attention to the ways the Lord
reveals himself to you in these Advent days.

O King of the nations, so long desired, cornerstone
uniting humankind,
come and save the work of your creation.
For the grace of attention to the ways the Lord
reveals himself to you in these Advent days.

O Emmanuel, God present in our midst, long
awaited Savior and King,
come and save us, O Lord our God.
For the grace of attention to the ways the Lord
reveals himself to you in these Advent days.

May the light of Christ shine on you and your loved
ones during this Holy Season.

– In His love, Timothy B. Brown, S.J.

God of our life,
there are days when the burdens we carry
chafe our shoulders and weight us down;
when the road seems dreary and endless,
the skies grey and threatening;
when our lives have no music in them,
and our hearts are lonely,
and our souls have lost their courage.
Flood the path with light,
turn our eyes to where the skies are full of
promise; tune our hearts to brave music;
give us the sense of comradeship
with heroes and saints of every age;
and so quicken our spirits
that we may be able to encourage
the souls of all who journey with us
on the road of life, to your honor and glory.

—Answered Prayers—

Kevin Hurley, a former student of mine, called home to talk about his first two weeks at Notre Dame. He had a great roommate. Howard Hall was the best dorm on campus. He told his parents of a party he was going to that Saturday night at St. Mary's — the women's college across the road from Notre Dame.

Two days later, early Sunday morning the phone rang at 6 am at the Hurley's house back in Boston. Mr. Hurley took the call. He listened without moving and tears came to his eyes. By the time Mrs. Hurley ran to the extension, Fr. Gene Gorski, the rector of Howard Hall, had turned the phone over to the doctor. Kevin's parents were told— closed head injuries, severe pulmonary contusion, slit pelvis, severe injury to left leg.

The night before, Kevin and his roommate had been walking back from St. Mary's. As they crossed the four lanes of US 31 between Notre Dame and St. Mary's, they heard the roar of an engine. Kevin's roommate had time to see a red car and jumped out of the way; but the car hit Kevin, hurling him across the road. And the car kept going– a hit and run.

The doctor told the Hurleys to come to South Bend on the next available flight. But he had little hope that Kevin would be alive when they arrived. That afternoon the Hurleys arrived at the surgical intensive care unit of South Bend Memorial Hospital. Steel pins and bars held their son's pelvic region together. The doctors had shaved Kevin's head and drilled a hole into his skull to measure the pressure on his brain. The regular ventilator wasn't enough, and fearing that Kevin would die the doctors put Kevin on a high frequency jet ventilator. Then the waiting began. One hour at a time. The simple fact was that Kevin was still alive though in a coma.

The doctors told the Hurleys not to expect too much. The odds were not good. Later that week Kevin's left leg would be amputated just below the knee.

Jesus, Our Beloved Protector has Fallen Asleep. But I am going there to wake him.

Kevin would have many visitors those dark days of September— the Notre Dame administration, campus workers, professors, priests and dozens of students from Notre Dame and St. Mary's. Some went up to the intensive care unit, others waited in the lobby sending word up to the Hurleys that Kevin was in their prayers. Later that month a special mass would be celebrated for Kevin with almost a thousand students in attendance. Meanwhile Kevin remained in a coma.

A month went by and the doctors felt that Kevin, though still in a coma, was stable enough to be transferred to a hospital in Boston. In November Kevin would blink his eyes, and later that month would respond for the first time when a nurse asked him if it hurt when she lifted his arm — "yes".... And on November 24th Kevin came out of a coma.

Your Brother will rise again, Jesus assured him.

In December the Dean of Freshmen flew to Boston with a videotape that had been put together by the Freshmen class. Pictures of friends and his roommate, scenes of the Freshmen orientation mass and registration, beach parties, and the marching band and closed with all the Freshmen gathered in the Notre Dame stadium shouting "Hi Kevin!". And Kevin sat there in his wheelchair, watching the video, at times seeming interested, at other times staring blankly at the screen. Later in December, Kevin would begin to talk again. Progress was slow, but before long, Kevin began to get in and out of his *wheelchair, his feeding tube was removed, and he began to eat normally. By February, he began to recognize old friends. One day he asked his mother for a pencil and paper and wrote a letter to his sister Sheilah:*

Dear Sheilah,
Do you believe in Mr. G and JC (God and Jesus that is) I do. Please pray for me.
Love Kevin.

And all of us did. Every week at mass at the prayers of the faithful we remember Kevin in a special petition.

<u>*Lord if you had been there my brother would never have died.*</u>
A year later, Kevin enrolled as a part time student at Boston College taking the business law course I was teaching at the time.

I believe in miracles. I believe that the Lord continues to heal, continues to reach out his hand, continues to touch those who need his curing touch. I believe in the power of prayer.

Kevin's mother in thanking a group of Notre Dame alumni for their prayers and support said: "The greatest gifts are not those you can touch or see, but those from the heart. I can only hope everyone will share in the day when Kevin will be able to stand up and thank you as I am doing right now."

At the last Sunday mass I said in Boston before moving to Loyola, I witnessed something I'll never forget— Kevin got up, steadied himself, his father not too far behind, and walked up the aisle to receive Communion from me.

——Lord Lift Me——

Lord from this world's stormy sea,
Give your hand for lifting me.
Lord lift me from the darkest night
Lord lift me into the realm of light
Lord lift me from this body's pain
Lord lift me up and keep me sane
Lord lift me from the things I dread
Lord lift me from the living dead
Lord lift me from the place I lie
Lord lift me that I never die.

– David Adam, *The Edge of Glory*

strength

—Psalm 84—

1. How amiable are thy tabernacles, O Lord of hosts!

2. My soul longeth, yea, even fainteth for the courts of the Lord: my heart and my flesh crieth out for the living God.

3. Yea, the sparrow hath found an house, and the swallow a nest for herself, where she may lay her young, even thine altars, O Lord of hosts, my King, and my God.

4. Blessed are they that dwell in thy house: they will be still praising thee. Selah.

5. Blessed is the man whose strength is in thee; in whose heart are the ways of them.

6. Who passing through the valley of Baca make it a well; the rain also filleth the pools.

7. They go from strength to strength, every one of them in Zion appeareth before God.

8. O Lord God of hosts, hear my prayer: give ear, O God of Jacob. Selah.

9. Behold, O God our shield, and look upon the face of thine anointed.

10. For a day in thy courts is better than a thousand. I had rather be a doorkeeper in the house of my God than to dwell in the tents of wickedness.

11. For the Lord God is a sun and shield: the Lord will give grace and glory: no good thing will he withhold from them that walk uprightly.

12. O Lord of hosts, blessed is the man that trusteth in thee.

—Prayer of Philippine Duchesne—

Lord, you are the center in which I find rest.

Give me your arm to support me,
your shoulders to carry me,
your heart to lean upon,
your cross to uphold me,
your body to nourish me.

In you O Lord, I sleep and rest.

Soul of Christ, sanctify me.
Body of Christ, save me.
Blood of Christ, inebriate me.
Water from the side of Christ, wash me.
Passion of Christ, strengthen me.
O good Jesus, hear me.
Within your wounds hide me.
Do not allow me to be separated from you.
From the malevolent enemy defend me.
In the hour of my death call me,
and bid me come to you,
that with your saints I may praise you
forever and ever.

Amen.

– St. Ignatius

For years, I've been wondering why the first words of
the "Spiritual Exercises" are not the "Principle and
Foundation" that we usually pray first, but the "Anima
Christi," the short prayer that Ignatius did not write,
although he did make it famous. It was popular in the
16th century, but it goes back at least two hundred years
earlier. The reason this opens the "Exercises," I think, is
because from the very outset Ignatius wanted to let us
know very clearly that no psychology of how to make
good choices and decisions has integrity apart from a
faith-journey's immersion into the wounds of Christ.

Let's just for a moment remind ourselves of two of
the "Anima Christi's" most powerful metaphors— so
rich, complex, and paradoxical that they are better called
"conceits." "O good Jesus..., within your wounds hide
me": the Latin makes the meaning so much more
potent— "intra tua vulnera absconda me." Let me
secretly depart, even be kidnapped, into the dark red
flesh, your warm and living tissue, where you have been
made weak, sensitive— where you hurt for us out of love.
Let me live there, draw nourishment there, feast there,
make my decisions and choices from within there—
faith's hiding place. To do this— this is the power and
the glory.

And then there is "Blood of Christ, inebriate me."
In plain English, "make me drunk." What an
extraordinary play of images on the real presence of
Christ in the Eucharistic wine. Being drunk changes
our perceptions and our thinking. It releases inhibitions
and weakens defenses. It is often sinful. But to become

drunk on the blood of Christ, to have our perceptions and thinking changed like His, to lose our usual way of understanding reality so that it conforms to His divine mind— yes, this is being besotted, but with the purest of wines that, even now, we shall soon take as pure gift.

– Stephen Fields S.J.

— O Holy One —

O Holy One down deep in my heart
enable me to join You down deep in my heart

O Holy One down deep in my heart
enable me to know You down deep in my heart

O Holy One down deep in my heart
enable me to love You down deep in my heart

O Holy One down deep in my heart
enable me to follow You down deep in my heart

—A Prayer for Love—

Nothing is more practical than finding God,
i.e., than falling in love in a quite absolute final way.

What you are in love with, what seizes your
imagination, will affect everything.

It will decide what will get you out of bed in the morning,
what you will do with your evenings,
how you spend your weekends,
what you read,
who you know,
what breaks your heart,
and what amazes you with joy and gratitude.

Fall in love, stay in love, and it will decide everything.

– Padre Arrupe, S.J.

challenges

1. Bless the Lord, O my soul. O Lord my God, thou art very great; thou art clothed with honour and majesty.

2. Who coverest thyself with light as with a garment: who stretchest out the heavens like a curtain:

3. Who layeth the beams of his chambers in the waters: who maketh the clouds his chariot: who walketh upon the wings of the wind:

4. Who maketh his angels spirits; his ministers a flaming fire:

5. Who laid the foundations of the earth, that it should not be removed forever.

6. Thou coveredst it with the deep as with a garment: the waters stood above the mountains.

7. At thy rebuke they fled; at the voice of thy thunder they hasted away.

8. They go up by the mountains; they go down by the valleys unto the place which though hast founded for them.

9. Thou hast set a bound that they may not pass over; that they turn not again to cover the earth.

10. He sendeth the springs into the valleys, which run among the hills.

11. They give drink to every beast of the field: the wild asses quench their thirst.

12. By them shall the fowls of the heaven have their habitation, which sing among the branches.

13. He watereth the hills from his chambers: the earth satisfied with the fruit of thy works.

14. He causeth the grass to grow for the cattle, and herb for the service of man: that he may bring forth food out the earth;

15. And wine that maketh glad the heart of man, and oil to make his face to shine, and bread which strengthens man's heart.

16. The trees of the Lord are full of sap; the cedars of Lebanon, which he hath planted;

17. Where the birds make their nests: as for the stork, the fir trees are her house.

18. The high hills are a refuge for the wild goats; and the rocks for the conies.

19. He appointed the moon for seasons: the sun knoweth his going down.

20. Thou makest darkness, and it is night: wherein all the beasts of the forest do creep forth.

21. The young lions roar after their prey, and seek their meat from God.

22. The sun ariseth, they gather themselves together, and lay them down in their dens.

23. Man goeth forth unto his work and to his labour until the evening.

24. O Lord, how manifold are thy works! in wisdom hast thou made them all: the earth is full of thy riches.

25. So is this great and wide sea, wherein are things creeping innumerable, both small and great beasts.

26. There go the ships: there is that leviathan, whom thou hast made to play therein.

27. These wait all upon thee; that thou mayest give them their meat in due season.

28. That thou givest them they gather: thou openest thine hand, they are filled with good.

29. Thou hidest thy face, they are troubled: thou takest away their breath, they die, and return to their dust.

——Jeremiah 29:11——

I know what I am planning for you, says the Lord.
I have good plans for you, not plans to hurt you.
I will give you hope and a good future.

——Philippians 1:8——

I long for you all in the heart of Christ

On the evening of October 19th, 1996, on the way to my parent's house to celebrate my sister's birthday, I often remember about how I felt: life was great and I had so much to look forward to. I was almost finished medical school, had finally determined my field of practice, had just come from a wedding surrounded by a great group of friends, and was about to see my family, who were all happy and healthy. After four years of college at Loyola and 3 1/2 grueling years of medical school, things were finally starting to make sense and fall into place.

Knowing from a young age that I wanted to help people make their lives better, I often found myself confused between the ever present difficulty of balancing a career with a family. Aware that the medical field was a prime place for me to help people, I was troubled in deciding between medicine and nursing or physical therapy.

I decided to be a physician during a spring break outreach trip during my junior year. In Appalachia, I was faced with a need that I had never before encountered: wonderful, giving people with no access to medical care. One individual, Earl, whose floor and roof we completely rebuilt, was faced with severe medical problems including heart failure. This experience opened my eyes and made me realize that I needed to be a physician to actively make things better for those around me. I needed to give, and being a doctor seemed like the best way to do it.

Ever since that point, I had been plugging away at the University of Maryland Medical School. In the midst of what is widely regarded as 'the doctor's initiation period', my first two years of medical school tested my fortitude and courage in ways that I had never before experienced. Despite the insane hours, incredible stress and pressure to learn, I still kept my priorities in line, volunteering, spending time with my friends and family.

In fact, I made it through the first three years of medical school, as well as the majority of life, with few scars but many wonderful friendships and treasured experiences. If I had been asked to speak on "leadership in the face of adversity" a year ago at this time, I would have respectfully declined because I would not have been qualified.

On that Saturday night in October of 1996, while having dinner with my family, I vividly remember thinking to myself that life has treated me very well thus far. I was content. I was focused on finishing medical school and starting my residency.

On Sunday, October 20, at 6:45 in the morning, my life and my plans were slightly altered. Having just dropped my brother off at BWI Airport, I had returned to the city for my second trip to the airport that morning, this time driving a medical school classmate.

As I was getting out of my car to help her load her luggage into my trunk, I was struck by a drunk driver in a Trans-Am moving at 55 mph. Thrown 20 plus feet into oncoming traffic lanes, with my car tossed 50 feet in another direction, I began to pray the "Hail Mary" with the person that was holding me, who I discovered later was the drunk driver.

Moments later, paramedics arrived who quickly transported me to The Shock Trauma Center at the University of Maryland Hospital. The doctors first ensured that I was intact internally, then went on to repair my two shattered legs. By that afternoon, it was clear that my right leg, although all of the major bones were broken in multiple places, was intact and repairable. My left leg, however, was in much worse shape, with not only severe bone, but also extensive muscle and tissue damage.

After 12 surgeries, 40 plus units of blood and valiant efforts by the surgeons, I was left with the decision of whether to remain a below-the-knee amputee, and risk many more surgeries and months of not being able to walk, or go against the surgeon's wishes and opt for an above-the-knee amputation, which I felt would enable me to move on with my life and get out of the hospital more quickly. I selected the above-the-knee amputation.

During the 4th year of medical school, most students take two months to interview and recharge for the upcoming residency program. I spent those two months between Shock Trauma and rehab. Most students at this point are deciding where they want to perform their residency and start their life. I was re-learning how to walk.

While in the hospital, shortly before making the decision to have the above-the-knee amputation, I set three short-term goals for myself:

- Graduate from medical school the following May WITH my class
- Start my residency program WITH my class
- And last but not least, walk WITH my class at graduation.

I still am not fully convinced I am qualified to speak to you about leadership in the face of adversity, but I do know that I accomplished all three of these goals and even walked at graduation without a cane.

I don't think that what I have done is really that special. If I sat home feeling sorry for myself - what good would that do me or those around me?

This event certainly changed my life in ways that I am still encountering; both physically, emotionally and spiritually. I do not believe that I have done anything differently in overcoming this problem than I have in overcoming other problems in the past. The primary difference, I feel, is that the trials of the last year have forced me to reach within myself and find out what I am really all about.

I had always been in leadership positions throughout my years in school and have always tried to reach out to those around me, from volunteering at soup kitchens to being treasurer of my medical school class. If one would want to consider me as a leader, I would view myself to be a "behind the scenes" type of leader — leading by example as opposed to a highly visible — "all eyes on you" — type of leader.

I feel I am guided by certain core principles which have directed me through the last 26 years:

Determination, bordering on stubbornness, is what drives me to achieve the goals I set for myself. Ever since I can remember, I have been setting goals and working to attain those goals to the fullest. I was determined to help people — I became a doctor. I was determined to not be dependent on my family and friends after being released from rehab — I moved back to my apartment with three floors, a narrow staircase and no bathroom on the first floor. After everyone told me I was crazy for moving back to that apartment, it made me more determined to stay. Some of my closest friends were afraid that the accident would have changed me — I was and am determined to stay the same person.

Self-Reliance – To face the challenges that confront you every day, you must be confident in your own abilities and comfortable with yourself. Losing a limb is not only a physical debilitation, but also an emotional one. To overcome such an event requires not only inner strength, but a belief that you can prevail. This attitude should pervade all facets of life in order to overcome the hurdles that we face daily, as well as the big "life" obstacles.

Trust in Others – Knowing when to ask for help. As a fiercely independent person, it was difficult for me to ask others for help after the accident because I did not want to acknowledge that I had limitations inflicted upon me by the accident. Things that I had taken for granted for years — from cooking dinner to hanging pictures on my bedroom wall — now were very difficult. I was the person who others had always asked for help. I learned through this process that asking for help, and trusting in others is not a sign of weakness. Rather, knowing and acknowledging your weaknesses and limitations I found to be an ultimate source of strength.

Positive Outlook – I have always accepted that things could and will go wrong in this life - but I believe in the proverbial "silver lining" in everything. At times, I get frustrated and fall into self-pity. I lost my leg and my life is irrevocably changed by this. But when I start to feel sorry for myself I try to think about where I have been and how fortunate I am. I am not lucky to be an amputee, but I am fortunate to be alive.

Humility – Since the accident I have tried not to focus on "why did this happen to me?," but rather, "Since it did happen, how can I learn from it and how can this experience help me help others?" I believed before, and continue to believe that there is nothing that will come my way that God and I cannot overcome. If this is his plan, then I need to find out my role within it.

Truly humbling has been the outpouring of support I have received. In fact, so many people wanted to visit me while in the hospital, that they had to put me under an alias — Renee Trooper — the last name because I was 'such a Trooper.'

Reaching Out to Others – I believe that experiences, both good and bad, are wasted if they are not shared with others. I would have never asked for this experience to happen, but it has. And I can't change that. While some may view this as a terrible thing, if I can touch others' lives, maybe even prevent similar occurrences or share my experiences with those who have gone through similar things, as I am trying to do by setting up an amputee visitation group in Lancaster General Hospital, where I am currently in residency, then I am doing my part to turn a tragedy into a triumph for myself and others.

Most of all, the challenges I have faced in the last year forced me to confront my own mortality and allowed me to appreciate all that I have. Saying that I have a newfound respect for life and its wonders would not do justice to my feelings. When in the hospital, I yearned for the life that I lost on that fateful October morning. I remembered running, jumping, dating, even walking with two legs and it made me sad.

A year later, I am running, rope climbing, walking, and am going skiing in a few months. I have accepted the trials that have been placed in front of me as God's will, and I have tried to embrace life with a fervor that I did not know prior to the accident. I suppose I know now that life really could be too short not to do this.

It is through this experience that I have discovered who I am — not who I am not. I have gained a deep appreciation for what I have as opposed to a yearning for what I do not.

You know, when the accident occurred, many people were afraid that my cheerful and bright disposition and outlook might be changed from the experience. They underestimated my determination and stubbornness — the drunk driver took my leg, but he has not, and will never get any more.

— Marie VanDebosche
Loyola College '93
Speech given to Loyola student body

—Irish Blessing—

May we have enough hope to keep us happy
Enough happiness to keep us smiling
Enough trials to keep us strong
Enough failure to keep us humble
Enough success to keep us eager
Enough friends to give us comfort
Enough wealth to meet our needs
And enough faith in ourselves, our business
and our country to banish depression.

Amen.

Gracious Lord and sweet Savior, give me a pure intention, a clean heart, and a regard to thy glory in all my actions.

Jesus, possess my mind with thy presence and ravish it with thy love, that my delight may be to be embraced in the arms of thy protection.

Jesus, be thou light unto mine eyes, music to mine ears, sweetness to my taste, and contentment to my heart.

Jesus, I give thee my body, my soul, my substance, my fame, my friends, my liberty, and life; dispose of me and all that is mine as shall be most to thy glory.

Jesus, I am not mine, but thine; claim me as thy right, keep me as thy charge, love me as thy child.

Jesus, fight for me when I am assaulted, heal me when I am wounded, revive me when I am spiritually killed, receive me when I fly, and let me never be quite confounded.

Jesus, give me patience in trouble, humility in comfort, constancy in temptations and victory against my ghostly enemies.

Jesus, give me modesty in countenance, gravity in my behavior, deliberation in my speeches, purity in my thoughts, righteousness in my actions.

Jesus, be my sun in the day, my food at the table, my repose in the night, my clothing in nakedness, my succor in all needs.

Jesus, let thy blood run in my mind as a water of life to cleanse the filth of my sins and to bring forth the fruit of life everlasting.

Jesus, stay mine inclinations from bearing down my soul, bridle mine appetites with thy grace, and quench in me the fire of all unlawful desires.

Jesus, keep mine eyes from vain sights, mine ears from hearing evil speeches, my tongue from talking unlawful things, my senses from every kind of disorder.

Jesus, make my will pliable to thy pleasure and resigned wholly to thy providence and grant me perfect contentment in that which thou allottest.

O Lord, make me strong against occasions of sin and steadfast in not yielding to evil, yea, rather to die than to offend thee.

Jesus, make me ready to pleasure all, loath to offend any, gentle in speaking, courteous in conversation, loving to my friends, and charitable to mine enemies.

Jesus, forsake me not, lest I perish; leave me not to mine own weakness, lest I fall without recovery.

Jesus, grant me an earnest desire to amend my faults, to renew my good purposes, to perform my good intentions, and to begin afresh in thy service,

Jesus, direct mine intention, correct my errors, erect my infirmities, protect my good endeavors.

Jesus, allay my passions and make me able to master them, that they never draw me beyond the rule of reason and piety.

Jesus, make me humble to my superiors, friendly to my equals, charitable to my inferiors, and careful to yield due respect to all sorts.

Jesus, grant me sorrow for my sins, thankfulness for thy benefits, fear of thy judgments, love of thy mercies, and mindfulness of thy presence.

Amen.

— Robert Southwell, S.J.

—Prayer of St. Francis de Sales—

Do not look forward
to what might happen tomorrow.
The same Everlasting Father
Who cares for us today,
will take care of you tomorrow and every day.
Either He will shield you from suffering
or He will give you
unfailing strength to bear it.
Be at Peace then and put aside
all anxious thoughts and imaginations.

renewal

1. Have mercy upon me, O God, according to thy loving kindness: according unto the multitude of thy tender mercies blot out my transgressions.

2. Wash me thoroughly from mine iniquity, and cleanse me from my sin.

3. For I acknowledge my transgressions: and my sin is ever before me.

4. Against thee, thee only, have I sinned, and done this evil in thy sight: that thou mightest be justified when thou speakest, and be clear when thou judgest.

5. Behold, I was shapen in iniquity; and in sin did my mother conceive me.

6. Behold, thou desirest truth in the inward parts: and in the hidden part, thou shalt make me to know wisdom.

7. Purge me with hyssop, and I shall be clean: wash me, and I shall be whiter than snow.

8. Make me to hear joy and gladness; that the bones which thou has broken may rejoice.

9. Hide thy face from my sins, and blot out all mine iniquities.

10. Create in me a clean heart, O God; and renew a right spirit within me.

11. Cast me not away from thy presence; and take not thy holy spirit from me.

12. Restore unto me the joy of thy salvation; and uphold me with thy free spirit.

13. Then will I teach transgressors thy ways; and sinners shall be converted unto thee.

14. Deliver me from bloodguiltiness, O God, thou God of my salvation: and my tongue shall sing aloud of thy righteousness.

15. O Lord, open thou my lips; and my mouth shall shew forth thy praise.

16. For thou desirest not sacrifice; else would I give it: thou delightest not in burnt offering.

17. The sacrifices of God are a broken spirit: a broken and a contrite heart, O God, thou wilt not despise.

18. Do good in thy good pleasure unto Zion: build thou the walls of Jerusalem.

19. Then shalt thou be pleased with the sacrifices of righteousness, with burnt offering and whole burnt offering: then shall they offer bullocks upon thine altar.

I think that perhaps the greatest pruning is the wounding of our own hearts, allowing to be vulnerable, open to being wounded.

Reconciliation "trims us clean" of resentment, bitterness, and makes us more untied and conformed with the One who made the interconnectedness of all things a reality in her own being, reconciling all, making all One, one Vine whose sap is the blood and water flowing from His heart through the branches.

– Clare Pratt, R.S.C.J.

—Irish Blessing—

My heart – created out of the living God
Christ's is the seed and Christ's is the harvest
May he gather us all in his barn
Christ's is the sea and Christ's is the fish
May his net embrace us all.

——*Prayer of Rev. Francis X. Knott, S.J.*——

Lord Jesus, through the power of the Holy Spirit,
Go back into my memory as I sleep.
Every hurt that has ever been done to me,
    heal that hurt.
Every hurt that I have ever caused to another person,
    heal that hurt.
All the relationships that have been damaged in my
    whole life that I am not aware of,
    heal those relationships.
But, Lord, if there is anything that I need to do,
If I need to go to a person because he or she is still
    suffering from my hand,
Bring to my awareness that person.
I choose to forgive, and I ask to be forgiven.
Remove whatever bitterness may be in my heart, Lord,
    And fill the empty spaces with your love.

Amen.

—Naked Crabs—

At the seashore, every pool and puddle left by the retreating tide seems to have a crab in it. Little ones scuttle sideways, squeezing under rocks, peeking from a patch of seaweed, occasionally venturing out to nibble on unwary human toes.

Now and then, you may see bigger crabs, in deeper, safer pools. With ponderous majesty, they wave huge claws as a warning to stay away.

On the beach, shells of crabs lie washed up by waves. Some are from crabs that died; others are simply discarded, a dwelling too small for its growing occupant. That's how crabs grow bigger—when their shells get too tight, they split open and grow a new one.

I've never talked with a crab, but I imagine the process of splitting open a shell must be painful. I'm sure that until they grow a new shell, they feel terribly defenseless and vulnerable. Because that's how we humans feel, when we crack open our shells.

Our shells aren't visible, like crabs', but they are there just the same—shells formed by years of habit that protect us from other people, shells that are the roles we play as parents, or children or bosses, or employees.

Every now and then we crack our shells open and emerge into a new world, quivering and defenseless.

Teenagers do it as they become adults. No wonder they get crabby sometimes. Adults do it as they learn to quit running their kids' lives. Or when they get laid off at work. Or when a wife or husband dies and they have to start over again, alone. When an investment fails, when a dream disappears.

In all these traumas of life, a shell is being broken…a new, vulnerable life is started.

Like a crab, the longer that shell has been growing around us, the harder it is to break open, to start again. The more painful the breaking becomes.

Some of our shells we have worn for generations. Our Christian faith can be a shell handed down by our ancestors. Some faith shells are worth keeping. Others may have become prisons- shells so encrusted with the barnacles of the past, so burdened with trailing weeds, so constricting, that we can no longer move when God calls.

No one looks for painful experiences in life or in faith. To avoid pain, we may prefer to stay locked into shells that no longer fit very well, rather than risk the vulnerability of cracking them open.

But when a crab's shell becomes too thick, too protective, too tough to crack open and start again, then the crab can't grow any more. That's when it dies. So do we!

– Anonymous

—A Prayer For Awakening—

Lord, may your love play upon my voice
and rest in my silence.
Let it pass through my heart,
into all that I do.
Let your love shine like stars in the
darkness of my sleep,
and in the dawn at my awakening.
Let it bum in all the flames of my desires,
and flow in all the currents of my love.
Let me carry your love in my life,
as a harp does its music,
and given it back to you at last with my life.

                                            – Tagore

For the past decade, some students from Loyola University in Baltimore, Maryland, have spent their January break in Tecate and Tijuana in an enormously successful venture called Project Mexico. One year twenty-five of us spent ten days working on two construction projects: one at a Catholic boys' orphanage conducted by a remarkable group of Mexican nuns, the other in a relatively new area of Tijuana, where we helped build a kitchen-cafeteria at which children can receive one hot meal a day for about a dollar. The hope is that the cafeteria will serve as a community center for people to share goods, food, clothing, and friendship.

Here is how one student described Project Mexico: "The project is a way of opening our eyes and hearts to global realities. We begin, many of us, as young people without an understanding of the full scope of human existence. In Mexico we discover first-hand the hard fact of extreme poverty. But the greatest discovery experienced is the compassion and kindness within the human spirit."

An instance of "opening our eyes and hearts" to "the hard fact of extreme poverty" is the following. In Mexico that year we visited a group of people in one of the colonias or "settlements." They have a tradition that on the feast of the Three Kings the children prepare a Christmas pageant, which is very important to all the people. Imagine that the poor, simple, smiling children in this obscure Mexican village shared the same sense of wonder and joy over their baby Jesus as did the shepherds and Magi 2,000 years ago.

As we know from the Gospel of Luke, no true homage to the birth of Jesus would be complete without a manger scene, and here in this village the manger scene was key to the whole

Three Kings celebration. All the children played their parts, from Mary and Joseph to the shepherds. The three Wise Men, the innkeeper, and even the animals turned out to be the real thing. And a cat, some chickens, and a few stray dogs also helped to form the backdrop.

As you picture this scene, you must not forget that these children were, in a real sense, materially very poor. The makeshift costumes worn that day were thrown-away clothes, rags pieced together. As the pageant unfolded, the children began praying and singing, and crowding closer and closer to the baby Jesus. The baby was a tiny creature a few months old, a beautiful baby boy clothed in rags. The other niños were practically on top of the child. I looked at the dirty ground, the animals sidling up to the infant, and then it struck me: this child—poor, dressed in rags, nearly helpless—he was the baby Jesus. This was probably truer to the actual setting and circumstances into which Jesus was born than any I had ever experienced. And that day I learned more about the reality of God's trusting love, his giving his Son over to the world and to Mary.

Of my last Project Mexico experience, I have several vivid, recurring recollections. One is of a small boy who dreamed of becoming an architect. Although I cannot remember his name, I am still troubled by the thought of him. I admired his sense of future. In Mexico the people's daily struggles with poverty and despair leave very little time for dreams. The fact that this boy could fancy such a future was a testimonial to the madres who reared him. But there was no real opportunity for him to see his dream reach fruition, and this realization frustrated me. Most boys do not go to high school because their parents cannot afford the uniforms the schools require.

Such hopes can be built on gratitude. There is an ancient Aztec prayer that speaks of gratitude and the preciousness of life and its fleetingness. As the Aztecs thank their God for their life, they acknowledge that they are simply on loan to one another for a short time. They have a prayer that reads:

> Oh, only for so short a while
> You have lent us to each other,
> Because we take form in your act
> of drawing us.
> And we take life in your painting us,
> And we breathe in your singing us.
> But only for so short a while
> Have you lent us to each other.

Isn't seeing life as being on loan a great philosophy to hold? I think it helps us to be courageous, to take risks, to be adventurous and daring. When you look at life as being on loan, you look at things differently. You look at this loan for what it really is—pure gift, pure grace given to us from God. When you look at life as a loan, material things get put into perspective.

I once heard a wise Jesuit say that it is impossible to be grateful and unhappy at the same time. When I was in Mexico I could see what he meant. And I can remember hearing some Loyola students from that trip make similar observations. Two students of the group met Lupe and her son Federico, while volunteering at La Casa de Los Pobres (House of the Poor) in Tijuana. There needy people can receive two meals a day, groceries, clothing, and health care. During their time at the Casa, the students became close to Lupe and Federico. On their last night in Tijuana, before joining the rest of us in Tecate, they gave Federico a small bag of toys and money. But when they took him home that evening, Federico showed them an act of generosity and selflessness that few might expect from a seven-year-old. As soon as the little boy got into the house, he took the bag and the money and gave them to his mother to divide among the other children. That's the way everyone was. They help others before they help themselves. The philosophy that all is on loan seems to have taken hold there.

Another student who graduated last May had her own special story of a woman who deeply touched her. Lupita is the mother of Gustavo and Martín, two boys from the orphanage where we worked. They stayed at the orphanage because Lupita was too poor and too sick to care for them. Lupita lived in one of the poorest colonias in Tijuana where people stay in structures made of plastic, cardboard, tires, or whatever else they can find for shelter. Part of Project Mexico money that year went toward the construction of a new house for Lupita and her family. In her fifties, Lupita must travel down a steep hill to get water for cleaning and cooking, and despite her cancer, arthritis and high blood pressure, she must then carry the huge jugs back up the steep slope. When the small group of Loyola students went to visit Lupita for the first time, she greeted them with hugs, invited them into her house and offered them tea and coffee. She had little to offer but gave away what little she had. That kind of hospitality made a deep impression on the students.

This January, another group of Loyola students will leave for Mexico. They are able to make the trip because of the generosity and assistance of many people at the university. The support for this venture has been tremendous; I think it can be said that Loyola University has demonstrated a gratitude and *appreciation which mirrors that displayed by the Mexican people* — *"What you receive as a gift — give as a gift!"*

—A Prayer for True Self—

May I find my healing in this giving.
May I always accept God's will.
May I find my true self by living for others
in a spirit of sacrifice and suffering.
May I die more fully to myself,
and live more fully in You.

As I seek to surrender to the
Father's will, may I come to trust
that He will do everything for me.

— Fr. Walter Ciszek, S.J.

—Comfort Food—

Having a home-cooked meal can heal the heart in ways medicine cannot. My mother's Golfer Stew is a favorite recipe of mine to have when I need a reminder of the wholesomeness of childhood.

Golfer Stew

5 lbs stew beef
3 cans tomato paste
2 cans beef bouillon
1 cup bread crumbs
2 tablespoons of salt and pepper
1 bay leaf
2 lg onions
5 carrots
5 lg potatoes

Combine all ingredients

Cover

Bake at 250 degrees for 5 hours

– Ann Brown

Close your eyes. Half of the world disappears. We think most of what we see.

Think just one thought

Choose one word

Ordinary thoughts are like boats sitting on a river, so closely packed together that we cannot see the river that is holding them up.

Slow down. You will begin to see the space appearing between the boats.

Thoughts, memory, feeling

To look at the stream of consciousness going from the boats to the river.

Let the boats go, return to the sacred word.

Letting go

Not to depend on thoughts

God cannot be contained in thoughts

Receive the Lord

Sacred words or phrases

– Anonymous

salvation

1. He that dwelleth in the secret place of the most High shall abide under the shadow of the Almighty.

2. I will say of the Lord, He is my refuge and my fortress: my God; in him will I trust.

3. Surely he shall deliver thee from the snare of the fowler, and from the noisome pestilence.

4. He shall cover thee with his feathers, and under his wings shalt thou trust: his truth shall be thy shield and buckler.

5. Thou shalt not be afraid for the terror by night; nor for the arrow that flieth by day;

6. Nor for the pestilence that walketh in darkness; nor for the destruction that wasteth at noonday.

7. A thousand shall fall at thy side, and ten thousand at thy right hand; but it shall not come nigh thee.

8. Only with thine eyes shalt thou behold and see the reward of the wicked.

9. Because thou hast made the Lord, which is my refuge, even the most High, thy habitation;

10. There shall no evil befall thee, neither shall any plague come nigh thy dwelling.

11. For he shall give his angels charge over thee, to keep thee in all thy ways.

12. They shall bear thee up in their hands, lest thou dash thy foot against a stone.

13. Thou shalt tread upon the lion and adder: the young lion and the dragon shalt thou trample under feet.

14. Because he hath set his love upon me, therefore will I deliver him: I will set him on high, because he hath known my name.

15. He shall call upon me, and I will answer him: I will be with him in trouble; I will deliver him, and honour him.

16. With long life will I satisfy him, and shew him my salvation.

The world is much in need of repair. The traditional spiritual word— reparation. To repair means to bring God's heart and our hearts together front and center. Through the Heart of Christ— the Sacred Heart— we find solace, rest, consolation, kindness and compassion. Christ resides in the heart of those who seek Him out. Prayer springs from that heart untied with Christ's heart.

Karl Rahner, a Jesuit theologian, once wrote that the priest of the 21st century would be a man with a pierced heart from which he would draw a lot of strength to do the work of the Lord. A pierced heart is one that has experienced sadness, a feeling of failure. But a pierced heart united with the Heart of Christ is strengthened by the knowledge of Christ's fidelity and compassion.

In him we were also chosen, destined in accord with the purpose of the One who accomplishes all things according to the intention of his will.

It's in Christ that we find out who we are and what we are living for. Long before we first heard of Christ and got our hopes up, he had his eye on us, had designs on us for glorious living, part of the overall purpose he is working out in everything and everyone.

—Mass of the Holy Spirit Homily—

Homily given at Wheeling Jesuit University,
September 11, 2003

Come, Holy Spirit, fill the hearts
of your faithful and kindle in them
the fire of your love.

A wise Jesuit once told me that before speaking at a big event, think of yourself as the body at an Irish wake. Everyone presumes you'll be there for the party, but no one expects you to say a whole lot. I was advised by Father Stark to keep my remarks short, and I'll do whatever I can to oblige him. Knowing him, I think you know what I mean.

My question today is how do we experience the Holy Spirit working within us right now? Let me begin with an image:

Years ago in Ireland, there was a process of burying warm coals in ashes at night in order to preserve the fire for the cold morning to come. Instead of cleaning out the cold hearth, people preserved yesterday's glowing coals under beds of ash overnight in order to have fast-starting new fire the next day. The process is an extremely important one. Otherwise, if the coals go out, a whole new fire must be built and lit when morning comes, an exercise that takes precious time and slows the more important work of the new day. The primary concern, then, was that the fire from yesterday not be permitted to burn out completely at the end of the day. On the contrary, coals hidden from sight under heaps of ash through the long, dark night were tended carefully so that the fire could leap to life again at first light. The old fire did not die;

it kept its heat in order to be prepared to light the new one."
(Joan Chittister, The Fire in These Ashes, *Kansas City: Sheed & Ward, 1995, pp. 36-37)*

Come, Holy Spirit, fill the hearts
of your faithful and kindle in them
the fire of your love.

I'd like for you to think of these coals as the coals of our own Jesuit tradition here at Wheeling – the coals of faith going back to 1954 when the school was founded, the coals of hope, and the coals of justice and peace. Back to the question, the question today is how we experience the Holy Spirit in our lives this day, September 11, 2003.

The paradox of our faith and with most enterprises in life is that when we give something, we lose it. When we keep something back, we have it. But with the Holy Spirit, it is just the opposite. Each of us only has what we have given away, and what we have kept back, we have lost.

That is the Holy Spirit. That is the tradition upon which the College was founded. The coals of faith and hope. The coals of justice and peace.

The Holy Spirit helps us to be generous, the Holy Spirit helps us to be aware of the ways in which the measure of what you have given is what you now have.

September 11th two years ago, I found myself facing a classroom of students stunned, looking at me without any sense of hope or future. I myself wasn't sure how to begin to address the meaning of that day. So I stood there praying to the Holy Spirit, asking for guidance and thought to myself that one thing I can do is talk about the three times in my own life that were similar to that day.

So I told them about Friday, November 22nd, 1963– the day that John F. Kennedy was assassinated. No reaction. Then I talked very personally about a very difficult time in my own life– the day I came home from work on a hot August day with a letter waiting to tell me whether or not I would be drafted to go to Viet Nam. No reaction. The third, when I did get some reaction, was when I told them about the afternoon I met with a doctor who told me that I had cancer, and would be having surgery immediately that evening, and no guarantees. That did get a bit of a reaction, but still not enough to get a conversation going.

So then I thought for a minute and what I could do was ask everybody to take a minute to be quiet. We did so and then I asked the students to tell me what emotion was going through their minds and their hearts at that moment. As we registered those emotions I realized that I had a real challenge. Emotions ranged from anger to fear to hatred to despair.

Finally one young junior said very quietly, "Father, I will never bring children into this world. I will never put anybody through what we are going through right now." That's when I knew that I had to say something. So I said, "This is your homework assignment and I want you to begin it now and take it home and bring it back next class. I want you to sit down and write a letter to your son or daughter, talking about the meaning of September 11th in your own life. And I want you to pour out your emotions and all the things that are going through you right now. And I want you to record them for your own children."

It kind of stunned them for a minute, but I realized it did shake them back into some reality, possibly that the world would go on. When I returned two days later to receive these letters, I'll never forget the letter I received from one student, an ROTC freshman, who wrote the letter that I pray all of us could write about our lives and our world that day. He talked about faith, he talked about peace, he talked about justice, and he called on the meaning of the power of Martin Luther King, Jr., who said, "We cannot allow this kind of hatred to consume us. We must move forward in peace." I knew then that the Holy Spirit was with us.

St. Augustine talks about hope as the most important of the three theological virtues, and hope has two lovely daughters: courage and anger. Courage, so that what can be, will be. And anger, so that what should not be, will not be.

One of the practices that we established at Loyola with our Alpha program — our first year program — is to teach the students the Examen. It is a very simple set of questions that we ask the students to work through three or four times a week and to get back in their journals with us. And so one on one I would sit down and find out three questions that these students would ask:

1) What are you grateful for?
2) What do you regret?
3) What are you going to do differently the next day?

As that semester went by you see those three questions begin to take a life of their own, naming all kinds of things to be grateful for, especially in light of 9/11 — family, health, security, and life. Regret oftentimes was about how a student didn't spend his time very well during the day — the waste of time. Generally that was a very big point that students made. And what we're going to do differently is where hope comes in. The Examen was such a big part of their experience in light of 9/11. I think it shaped them in new ways.

Whatever is true,
Whatever is honorable,
Whatever is right,
Whatever is pure,
Whatever is lovely,
Whatever is of good repute,
Dwell in those things

—Irish Blessing—

Deep peace of the running wave to you.
Deep peace of the flowing air to you.
Deep peace of the quiet earth to you.
Deep peace of the shining stars to you.
Deep peace of the gentle night to you.
Moon and stars pour their beaming light on you.
Deep peace of Christ, the light of the world, to you.

—Matthew 11:28-29—

Come to me,
all you who are weary.
I will refresh you, for I am gentle
and humble of heart.

preservation

1. I will lift up mine eyes unto the hills, from whence cometh my help.

2. My help cometh from the Lord, which made heaven and earth.

3. He will not suffer thy foot to be moved: he that keepeth thee will not slumber.

4. Behold, he that keepeth Israel shall neither slumber nor sleep.

5. The Lord is thy keeper: the Lord is thy shade upon thy right hand.

6. The sun shall not smite thee by day, nor the moon by night.

7. The Lord shall preserve thee from all evil: he shall preserve thy soul.

8. The Lord shall preserve thy going out and thy coming in from this time forth, and even for evermore.

—*A Prayer for Kindness*—

Keep us, O God, from all pettiness.
Let us be large in thought, in word, indeed.
Let us be done with fault-finding and
leave off all self-seeking.
May we put away all pretense and meet
each other face to face, without self pity
and without prejudice.
May we never be hasty in judgment,
and always be generous.
Let us always take time for all things
and make us to grow calm, serene and gentle.
Teach us to put into action our better
impulses, to be straightforward and unafraid.
Grant that we may realize that it is the
little things of life that create differences,
that in the big things of life, we are as one.
And, O Lord God, let us not forget to be kind!

Amen.

– Janet Stuart R.S.C.J.

—Power and Wonder of the Holy Spirit—

During my time as Jesuit Provincial of Maryland, I wrote many letters. Here is one I wrote keeping in mind the Power and Wonder of the Holy Spirit.

Dear Brothers in Christ,

This time of year we are bringing some things to a close for the season– our academic institutions, for instance– and entering into the more relaxed season of summer. The men who have been studying for the priesthood for so many years are finishing their studies and we will soon celebrate with them their ordination. We take time to pause and celebrate the lives of our Jubilarians. The season of Easter is similarly drawing to a close with Pentecost. How do we name the Holy Spirit whose presence is felt in all these activities? How do we continue to be converted to God at the core of our being? How do we become persons of the Holy Spirit?

It is the Holy Spirit that pours this aspiration for holiness into our heads, into our hearts, into our souls. And the measure of your holiness, the measure of my holiness, will be Jesus. Holiness is a way of living one's life. A way of seeing one's life, and thinking about one's purpose.

In John's Gospel the Spirit is called the Paraclete. There is no exact English translation for the Greek Paraclete. Sometimes it is translated as advocate— someone who speaks for another; sometimes it is translated as defender— someone who acts on one's behalf, one's counselor. But perhaps the closest we can get to the meaning of the word is the one who spurs runners on in a race. The Paraclete is like an athlete's trainer. The Paraclete stands at the side of the track and encourages the runners. You can do it, go for it, go for the gold. Paraclete is the spur, that driving vision; the Spirit is the one who pushes us. The image takes off!

The ministry of the Holy Spirit never erases our desires or our capacity to desire; the Holy Spirit helps us to shape our desires. And, according to Ignatius, there can be no greater desire than the desire to be with and like Jesus:

Whenever the praise and glory of the Divine Majesty would be equally served, in order to imitate and be in reality more like Christ our Lord, I desire and choose poverty with Christ poor, rather than riches; insults with Christ heavy with them, rather than fame; I desire to be accounted as worthless and a fool for Christ, rather than esteemed as wise and prudent in this world.

Bernard of Clairvaux called the Holy Spirit the kiss of God. St. Hildegarde saw the Holy Spirit as the "breast-plate of life, girdle of beautiful energy." The Nicene Creed refers to the Spirit as the Lord and Giver of Life. Other images are found in the Litany of the Holy Spirit: Consuming Fire, Burning Love, Author of All Good. The Curé of Ars saw the Spirit "Like a mother leading by the hand her child." Dietrich Bonhoeffer considered the Spirit to be the "Pledge of the abiding presence of Jesus."

How do we name the Spirit? Are we willing to surrender ourselves to the Spirit, receiving the grace of encouragement to become utterly enthralled with God through Jesus? Do we allow ourselves to be guided by the Holy Spirit? Do we allow ourselves to live in God's love and allow that love to live in us? When we do, we become something more. We become people conformed to the image of Christ. Ignatius understood this and provided us with the tools to stir up our love of God to the point of being enthralled through the Exercises.

Be assured of my continued prayers for each of you. Through the Spirit God's love is poured into each of our hearts. In that love we can more fully understand who Christ is, what Christ does. Through that love we can be further drawn to a complete enthrallment with God, accepting and cherishing this great gift we have been given.

Yours in Christ,
Timothy B. Brown, S.J.
Provincial

—Prayer of St. Francis of Assisi—

Remember that when you leave this earth,
you can take nothing you have received...
but only what you have given;
a full heart enriched by honest service,
love, sacrifice and courage.

St. Patrick's Hymn at Evening

O Christ, Son of the living God,
May your holy angels guard our sleep.
May they watch us as we rest
And hover around our beds.
Let them reveal to us in our dreams
Visions of your glorious truth,
O High Prince of the universe,
O High Priest of the mysteries.
May no dreams disturb our rest
And no nightmares darken our dreams.
May no fears or worries delay
Our willing, prompt repose.
May the virtue of our daily work
Hallow our nightly prayers.
May our sleep be deep and soft,
So our work be fresh and hard.

—Near to the Heart of God—

There is a place of quiet rest
Near to the heart of God
A place where sin cannot molest
Near to the heart of God.

O Jesus, Blest Redeemer, sent
Near to the heart of God
Hold us, who wait before thee,
Near to the heart of God.

There is a place of comfort sweet,
Near to the heart of God
A place where we our Savior meet,
Near to the heart of God.

There is a place of full release,
Near to the heart of God
A place where all is joy and peace
Near to the heart of God

– An African American Spiritual

—Evening Prayer—

Watch O Lord, with those who wake,
or watch, or weep tonight, and give your angels
and saints charge over those who sleep.
Tend your sick ones, O Lord Christ.
Rest your weary ones,
Bless Your dying ones.
Soothe Your suffering ones.
Pity Your afflicted ones,
shield Your joyous ones.
And all you're your love's sake.

– Irish Blessing

Conclusion

This book has been filled with stories of the heart- heart wrenching, heart breaking, heart felt. The heart is healed and becomes tender when it has the chance to hear and resonate to the vibrant stories of those closest to the Lord. Someone once described spirituality as the way the human heart tunes in. Listening to the beat of the heart in sync with the Heart of Christ has been a spiritual discipline of mine. The Psalms are the gateway to the Heart of God.

Pray the Psalms with your heart...listen to God's words as they echo within.

Remember what an old Brazilian Bishop said right before he died:

> At the end of the journey they will say to me:
>
> Have you lived?
>
> Have you loved?

And I without saying anything, will open my heart full of names.

> – Bishop Pedro Casadaliga

—Bibliography—

Houselander, Caryll. *The Reed of God*, London, Sheed &
Ward, Ltd., 1976.

Norris, Kathleen. *The Psalms with Commentary*, New York:
Riverhead Books, 1997.

The Holy Bible, King James Version.

Talented writers, innovative students, fresh minds at work.

Apprentice House is the country's only campus-based, student-staffed book publishing company. Directed by professors and industry professionals, it is a nonprofit activity of the Communication Department at Loyola University Maryland.

Using state-of-the-art technology and an experiential learning model of education, Apprentice House publishes books in untraditional ways. This dual responsibility as publishers and educators creates an unprecedented collaborative environment among faculty and students, while teaching tomorrow's editors, designers, and marketers.

Outside of class, progress on book projects is carried forth by the AH Book Publishing Club, a co-curricular campus organization supported by Loyola University Maryland's Office of Student Activities.

Eclectic and provocative, Apprentice House titles intend to entertain as well as spark dialogue on a variety of topics. Financial contributions to sustain the press's work are welcomed. Contributions are tax deductible to the fullest extent allowed by the IRS.

To learn more about Apprentice House books or to obtain submission guidelines, please visit www.ApprenticeHouse.com.

Apprentice House
Communication Department
Loyola University Maryland
4501 N. Charles Street
Baltimore, MD 21210
Ph: 410-617-5265 • Fax: 410-617-2198
info@apprenticehouse.com

CPSIA information can be obtained
at www.ICGtesting.com
Printed in the USA
FFHW01n2044180718
47485584-50776FF

9 781934 074800